This is a poem that sometimes gives us the middle finger, often laughs at its own broken face. To be young and white and suburban in America is often to walk that line between "badass and punkass." Weaving the memory of one Fourth of July night gone not too terribly wrong with conditional questioning, and narrative that leaps into the future, with social insights in language and syntax both colloquial and investigative, Les Kay has collaged a "motherfucker" of a book length poem which perfectly captures that space, of brash masculine recklessness and bravado, astonished by the wreckage nearly wrought, asking after the litany of collisions and losses, "Fuck, they were beautiful—/ how did we get here, there?"

Sean Thomas Dougherty, author of *All You Ask for is Longing: New and Selected Poems*

©2015
Lucky Bastard Press,
Oakland, CA

ISBN 978-0-9964099-1-9

All rights reserved
This book may not be reproduced, in whole or in part including illustrations, in any form (beyond that copying permitted by 107 and 108 of the U.S Copyright Law and except by reviewers for the public press), without written permission from the author/s

Cover art and book design ©2015 featuring Tony Tasse's sculpture "Eye" & back cover photo taken by Janine Curry in downtown Dallas, Texas

Badass

A poem by
Les Kay

That's just a toy, he said

And you pressed the cold nose of your

Palm-sized .22 to his forehead,

Try me, motherfucker.

Try me.

And fuck if it doesn't sound like

Whatever film we wanted to be like

But his slightly smarter friend

Yoked his hand to plaid sleeve

Yanked, yanked, *come on man*

Let's get the fuck

Outta here.

And they went

If they were puppies, their tails would've cupped their crotches.

Breath.

Breath of cigarette, of weed, of coke, of gasoline,

We all had a beer in the back of—yes—*his* truck, a tapped keg

Spouting forgetfulness in the nightshade bed behind amateur tint

That trembled, peeled in the intertwined tweeter and bass.

The night's still young

And I'm fucked-

Up...

Everyone.

Who knows if the swerve was him or you or us—miles and miles and miles from home—traveling highways, the pedals like water skis on tingling feet, feet becoming skis, slideskipping from tiny crest to crest, each touch of steering wheel slide, slide

And the road was water;

the water, asphalt;

the asphalt parted like Sea;

And Saul saw Jesus.

What were we on?

I don't want to glorify, pinup,

I don't want this to be

Another glossy poster, a piss-cup to keep

A bagboy job, a drive-thru job,

A job job that jobs you of your will

Did James lose his job?

I don't want to name names,

tell the truth, caution youth,

slather patchwork veneers over half-lived lives

I don't want to tell a fucking story it's not a fucking story.

This is a fuck poem. A try me motherfucker poem. A let's get the fuck out of here poem.

But Peter, he was our rock,

        Mostly sober, head enough

                To take us each

By the hand, ask,

        You ok? Man, you ok?

                We got to get outta here

You got to keep your cups down.

***

Downtown swerving down one-way metered streets,

Neon of brewpubs, jewelers, tattoo parlors, clubs,

Dancing through the pulse of streetlamp cone, stoplight halo,

Nowhere, nowhere, not there when a black man with bad teeth

Waved you into in an overfull lot,

Behind a camera shop—no a record store—

Said, *I'll watch your truck.* You—no, we—thought

He was homeless, handed him a five.

We weaved, tilted the chalk-scrawled, bottle-broken sidewalks,

Brushed hard against fraternity boys, their hairspray dates,

Watched a man, a woman (dizzy, peroxide) dive headfirst

Toward gravel lots to be tethered back into air.

We would have done the same if we had the money.

We walked several blocks several times looking—

If we had the money if we had the money if we had.

***

(Must the man with bad teeth be black?

We all had bad teeth—some still do.)

    Before the reveal

    Yes.

        (Revelation and another Paul

        Another island)

***

Let's get outta here

And we fell in line

Back to where we'd been,

But the lot empty, the truck gone, a tow truck driver

Strapped and chained a late

Model sedan against the flecked white paint

Of dented divot bed

And the driver pointed at the sign,

It's at the end of Elm.

[. . . . .] you said.

                (Erasure of fear—badass, badass, punkass

                      Longing to say

The unsayable

Twist, pop, maim, like cartilage of knee against fender for the sake of your story—BAD ASS—this is not your story. It's not their story...it's the story of a lovely lady...it's a story torn from the headlines...it's the greatest story ever told...it's a joke of a story....a chicken crossing a road...it's the south welling up inside you like semen...it's the fucking of the fucked....we're all fucked, Mary.)

[. . . . . .] you said.

   And we prayed, we [Peter,
Simon, Paul, John, Judas] lit Marlboro Reds with Zippos.

               We fell to our
               asphalt knees

   And we prayed, we wanderers
for night's salvation, for the fermentation

               Of all our
               tomorrows

   And we walked, on Nike-
pinched toes, the desert of Elm, higher than we'd

               Been before,
               believed.

And we walked our wandering,
sipping backwash of one last beer, easing

Along the
curve of road

Past the grass-green street signs
we knew into an unknown of 7-11s

Until signage
browned

The 12-ft. chain-link topped
with barbed wire coils, the still-open

Office,
the bluelit

      Payphone told we'd arrived, and
we sat on the curb, talking trash to each

          Other as you
          phoned

     Your mom and asked for a loan
on his behalf. And he begged to know

          His truck,
          like a child,

     Was unscathed, and they let us
send someone else to check, as he

          Stood by
          waiting

     For your mom.

Paul ducked
into the impound lot

Behind the
office. We lazed—

What was
said? I can't make this up—

Strutted
through the unlocked for him

Gate,
cradling the half-keg,

Like a stolen
television.

***

Was I not the one you loved most?

Was it not I who held your meditations

On the prospect of ceding life too soon

In the cradle of my cranium? Wasn't

It me who blessed and cursed the litany

Of seedling names you tried and tilled

With red pen, black marker? Didn't I

Weep with you when the names,

Names, names burst through the garden

Of what you thought possible?

Yet I was last to hear

(moving 2,000 miles without phone numbers)

Years later you volunteered

(500 miles later)

Bussed to San Diego to test yourself against the surf

To erase the self you'd known in the surf

(a self for sale, like any other)

To become one

(no such thing)

Of a unit

(no such thing)

To kill a man

(children, really)

On ancient sands, in poppy fields,

(you badass, you).

Hush, hush.

Shhhh . . .

Teach me the language of stealth

The sea snake strikes

Of serrated blade, filmic violence,

Tell me how it differs from TV,

To feel vertebrae crack

In your palms—

To feel Life, pulsing in your palms

As Necessity—cold, silence

Pops open into possible

Capture, your own End

Staring—blackened eyes,

Dripping seawater. Teach me,

My friend, your silent trade.

Hush, hush.

***

[By pre-established logic, we should build a passion. Here, a platter. There, thorns. An inversion. A tilted simulacra of the original. Good news stalling in parched throats. Stigmata, looped again and again like the final scene of a snuff film. Broken lives transcribed, refigured—a sort of plastic surgery on the face of history, the rhinoplasty and tummy tucks of the soon to one day be sainted. Tsk-tsk. St. Fuck Up, St. Outcast, St. Believe You Me & the outpouring of one day, the dissemination—whispers, letters, faxes, emails. Until their small bodies are as forgotten as what they said, until their small bodies, broken like a baby possum's back in the jowls of a hound, broken like a promise never promised, broken like earth. And upon that day, that one day of which we dream, families will drop their spades and halt their threshers, come in from the fields to feast, meager. And families will bless their hollowed names, attempting with a frequency approximating never to live lives of fastidious purpose. Only later, much later, will it be revealed that there was no purpose to their spurious wandering. Only later, much later, will it be revealed that there is nothing to reveal. Bodies of bone, bodies of blood—absence and aporia—they will have become (as we are becoming) the space in which we etch our fictions, the catch in a throat.]

[...]

[...]

[...]

***

The antidote is telling.

        Across the street

                Others gathered on roofs

We had missed the stadium

        Fireworks

                The ember cascade

Simulacrum of rocket and bomb

        Show of force

                Music and light, light and music

Missed the gathering

        The celebration

            Of country we loved.

XOXO

        SWAK

& SWAT

Oh, old glory, perforated in the night, ragtag ragamuffin cloth sewn on the sinews of sniper shots, improvised smallpox

Inoculations, Hessian guerilla tactics, foreign blockades,

    Native guides, invisible ink passed from pack to pack

Beneath redcoat noses, lucky breadsoup winters for troops

    Without shoes, freed servants with skin the color of

Stained oak, bayonets, sedition, and reams of quill-dipped

    Ink written by men who could care less about God,

Or Equality or Destiny, despite what rhetoric you may have

    Heard. War makes villains. War makes a finer fugue.

War makes and makes and makes, or why else, my love,

    Why else crawl through brush and foxhole, move over

The top, far from home, far from London Bridge, falling?

Down. And like the apostles there were

Twelve plus one spread among the heathens like disease,

Like us, drunk among the disease, spreading

Out to corners of the globe: Pittsburgh, Plattsburgh, Tikrit

And back to the places we'll call home,

Measuring hopes with thimbles pressed

Against the same pattern:

[Take the young, promise the unreachable. Take the young, before infants ensnarl. Take them. Let them believe fallacies. Let them reify their own fallacies of skin & language. Suspend. Erase with hut one two chant one two who you wanna screw one two sandcamos three four dressblues one two my love three four my love my love & bodyarmour three four my love.]

[Take the young.]

Why did Peter cross the road? *To get busted.*

Where's Peter's gun? *I don't know.*

How many cops does it take to buy a doughnut?

None.

They have guns.

***

No warrant out for Peter that night,

No handcuff chafe after slithering

Down a live oak, tossing the spent

Roman candle into the next lot,

Leaving his .22 perched between

Branches like an ornament black

Chrome and black as the red and blue

Gumball of PD, Five Oh, oh, oh

Filled half-drowsed retinas and glowed,

Glowed, glowed like something filmic.

         And the fireworks,

    fuck, they were beautiful.

How did we get here, there—

Old enough to vote or die,

Or owe or own, though not quite

To drink or to drink and drive—

Where did the skateboards,

Bicycles, fried-pie afternoons

Go? What tore Simon from

His studies and into stockroom,

Warehouse, delivery? How

Much does each of us need

To see again the fireworks

Exploding over Elm Street

Red as neon, green as Simon's

Eyes, blue as the San Diego

Sea where commanders

Tried to ~~drown~~ remake you?

O won't you please

                Take me

                              Home

Won't you please

                Swing low

                              Sweet, sweet chariot

O won't you please

                Make it, make it

                              Stop, stop, stop

Won't you please

                Please, please

                              Let me get what I want

O won't you please

                Please, please

Help me.

In the year that changed everything Simon's son—

Framed with hospital machines that curled tubing

Into his stuffed nostrils—surgery loomed—student

Loans no longer enough for back rent, for booties,

For three meals for his girlfriend, himself. She slept

Beside their son while Simon planned, left his studies,

Took another job, the night shift at a gas station,

Took another job, second shift at an insulation

Factory. His body, learning rote movements to

Keep his hands intact, his rent almost current, his light

Bill paid, his pantry jeweled, at least, with baby food

While his girlfriend slept in a straight-backed hospital

Chair. It only took two months until he called Paul

Again and again, and Paul agreed to bring him in

To front him a kilo, so long as he wouldn't talk.

He wouldn't, even when what he wore was not his,

Even when his thought was inscribed upon a body

No longer his own, even when the thought he thought

Was reaction until lights went out, as he wrote me

Once before, before his son severed from time,

Cleaved from cohesive narrative. One moment,

Dancing into first, awkward kiss, the next,

Donning a gown to take a diploma at Harvard,

Yes, Harvard, and such was how he slept, never,

So we believe, blaming Paul—or those of us by then

Too far from Huntsville to make the trip, to say

His name during visiting hours, or to think

His name during our vanishing hours that grew

Frequent as gray hairs, as we missed you and

Missed who we were when you were here. [...]

[Is the speaker Judas or John—or neither—neither Gnostic nor Catholic readings forbidden, so I must become indeterminate to remain beloved, confidant, betrayer, beloved remainder of indeterminacy from centuries so often deemed useless—or mere grafting upon a trellis, a prop chalice, a pixilated chalice, a mustard seed planted within a proverb—or are all readings forbidden—or is this unbending arc toward sacrifice only another artifice, another structure, another short cut, another system shredding its titanium skin and the skins of others?]

> And the road was fire;
>
> the fire, sandstorm;
>
> the sandstorm parted by shells;

And you saw [. . .]

What did they put you on?

> I don't want to want you back with us, I don't
>
> Want to want you back enough to pin another
>
> Medal to your chest, you badass, fucked up
>
> Fuckup standing up for glossy poster
>
> Country, nation that said it needed you.
>
> > *Did you need it too?*

I don't want to say this,

tell the truth, caution youth,

slather patchwork veneers   over half-lived lives

I don't want to tell a fucking story   it's not a fucking story.

This is a death poem. A try me deathfucker poem. A let's never get the fuck out poem.

***

While we wait for you

To return, to rise,

To take your mythic

Place, your symbolic

Curtain call, your

Friend returning from

Overseas embrace

(you won't)

While we scatter to other shores,

While we scatter ourselves,

While we wonder when the story ends,

When we remember the love for each other

(transient as jazz solos)

Where have I gone?

Have I betrayed you,

Myself, the others?

(yes)

Remember, remember, remember.

(why?)

Lest we forget, forget.

Behind the office. We lazed—

And from a rooftop on the other side of Elm Street, the explosions bright as television.

And black market fireworks, illegal in our county, arced over the street, clustering hues.

And we were fucked up, looking up, as the pop, pop, pop of simulation colored horizons.

And we watched, our fireworks having finally arrived cascading sparks over Elm.

And the 7-11 signage, like a flood light filled all our faces, all our faces.

And the police came and no one, that night, was arrested.

And now, now

    I want to take you back to those explosions

    And ask about the metaphors

    Hear the conversation slurred with whatever

        And ask about the stories

        Hear us teach each other what we know

        And tell our own stories

        (have I, as yet, come close)

Across the chasms, bridge the stories we have with the stories we need, like you, no longer necessary—

(no longer . . . [...])

And tell stories no one else can:

Once upon a time, there where bicycles, turtles caught in creeks, shooting baskets at the community center.

Once upon a time, there were walks to the library.

Once upon a time, there were skateboard quests through concrete storm gullies.

Once upon a time, there were futures,

                delimited

by where we were born,

the factories where our parents

[...]

[...]

[...]

***

The next day: *fines, fines, fines.*

Only out for a good time.

A pawnbroker's eye in a loupe.

Matthew's hand, vice on Paul's arm.

Everywhere light, how blessed we were not

To have killed anyone (ourselves) that night,

Would that the blessing lasted for you,

For all city boys like you who joined up,

Believing, too much, what they'd been

Told that year that changed everything—

Five wandering years from that firework night.

Fuck, they were beautiful.

Les Kay is the author of *The Bureau* (Sundress, 2015) and co-author of *Heart Radicals* (ELJ Publications, 2016). He holds a PhD with a focus on Creative Writing from the University of Cincinnati and an MFA from the University of Miami, where he was a James Michener Fellow. His poetry has appeared widely in journals such as *[PANK], Redactions, South Dakota Review, Southern Humanities Review, Sugar House Review, Whiskey Island,* and *The White Review*. He is also an Associate Editor for *Stirring: A Literary Collection*. He lives in Cincinnati, teaching writing, and caring for three very small dogs.

www.ingramcontent.com/pod-product-compliance
Lightning Source LLC
Chambersburg PA
CBHW051958290426
44110CB00015B/2299